The Essay Collection

mianneAbooks.com

What Is Wrong With Black People Today???

...I'll Tell You!!!

Because This Is A State Of Emergency!!!

1. **WE DO NOT KNOW ANYTHING ABOUT THE TRUE HISTORY OF OUR ANCESTORS, OUR KIDS ARE STILL ON THE STREETS SELLING DRUGS, WE MAKE UP MORE THAN HALF THE JAIL POPULATION IN AMERICA AND OUR FAMILY CIRCLE IS ONLY WEAKENING.** Every time I am out selling books, someone will tell me I need to come to their church. Being Godly is excellent and needed however it would be nice if we could talk about other things as well such as how the former prime minister of Britain Gordon Brown said Africa is the key to get out of the world recession? (Meaning, the world is going to come up off African's back yet the Africans on that land will still be poor because the world leaders will simply take the African's resources without giving Africans adequate pay! Read the article at www.bbc.co.uk/news/uk-10750077). How come more brothas aren't becoming scientists and chemists? We have tons of preachers...but we also need chemists and scientists and businessmen! Instead of talking to me about what church I need to go to (and once again, spirituality is very important, yet and still), why aren't these brothas and sistas also talking about the

current situation of Blacks, political issues, the Civil Rights Movement, how to better the educational institutions and what is currently going on in Africa? Why aren't our kids informed on our true history by their parents since we cannot expect the school systems to do it? Many Black American children today do not know anything about African culture! And many of us have never even taken an African Studies or Urban Studies course yet we spend tons of money on clothes, weave and clubbing! **YOU HAVE TO KNOW WHO YOU ARE BEFORE YOU CAN SUCCEED IN LIFE!**

2. **WE ARE ASAHMED OF WHO WE TRULY ARE!!!** We spend all this money on Remi hair and Indian hair. Awkward colored contacts on brothas and sistas that don't match their skin tones, brothas still talking about Red Bones and hatin' on dark skinned women (I am so sick of hearing people dog Serena, Venus and Beyonce. Meanwhile, the same ones praise Kim Kardashian and back in the day I heard many a Black man say he'd take J.Lo any day over Beyonce!) Why do we think anything mixed or non Black is better than our own Blackness? There is

nothing wrong with Kim Kardashian or J.Lo but there is nothing wrong with Venus or Serena either! We still go around talking about "the grade of hair" or who has "good hair." Why are we so ashamed of being Black??? **WE LOOK UP TO ANY OTHER RACE OTHER THAN BLACK!!! EVEN THE BLACKS WHO SAY THEY ARE PROUD TO BE BLACK GO AROUND TALKING ABOUT "GOOD HAIR." MANY OF US WANT TO PROCREATE WITH ANYONE OUTSIDE THE BLACK RACE SO THAT OUR KIDS WILL BE CONSIDERED "PRETTY."** Well, guess what? They did a study and you know what? In regards to Whites, Asians and Hispanics, Black were the last choice when choosing a marriage spouse. Then you have all these Black Folks talking about how they love The Dominican Republic! Did you know many Dominican Republic clubs ban Blacks and gays from entering their clubs? So why do we think anything else is prettier and better than Black when they certainly don't think we are all that? Because we have cultural and racial low self esteem!!! In the movie *Selena*, Selena's father makes her learn to sing in Spanish even though she did not want to learn Spanish at first. Selena's father told her that she had to know who she was and that when you try to be something you are not, people know it and can sense it. Black people, let's let our real hair out of these lacefont wigs, lift up those bad Remi weaves, let the napps breathe and raise that fist in the air!!! **Sidenote**: Now I have worn weaves in the past and have no problem with non-nappy hair, however, the issue is, we should also be able to respect the napps as well and not be ashamed to wear our own hair in its natural state even when it is not wavy or more European-like in texture. That's all I'm sayin'!

3. **WE NEED TO STOP SUCKING UP TO OTHER RACES AND ONLY RESPECT THOSE WHO RESPECT US!!!** We don't have to hate other races (many times it is the Arabic business man that allow me to sell my books in front of their business and I appreciate that. I do business with all races.) But we do need to love ourselves and not allow other races to diss us!

4. **WE MUST START PATRONING EACH OTHER!!!** When I am out, most Black people walk right by me and ignore me when I ask

them to check out the books I have written. Or, they ask me if I write Christian books. When I say I write about life, many of them don't want to check out my book catalog after that. Why is this a problem? Well, we as Black folks give everyone else our money. Arabs who are not Christian, celebrities who care nothing about us and don't even know our names and aren't Christian, we patron Whites stores, Jewish stores, Korean owned beauty supplies, Chinese restaurants with the Buddha up front—anything but Black owned businesses. But when someone like me asks some of us to check out my work, they walk right by me like I'm trash or demand that I be Christian before they can talk to me. (And I'm not against Christianity. I grew up in a Christian household). Question: Do us Black folk ask Meijer grocery store and the gas station and Bath and Body Works and Macy's if the store owners are Christian before spending money with them? NO! So why does it matter whether I am Christian or not before Black folks can check out the books I wrote? The "more educated" Negros and the gutter hood rats—they are good at ignoring a sista like me selling my work independently.

Many ask me why I'm out selling my books in the streets if I'm published. If they really knew about business, they'd respect what I do. Some authors only make pennies on the dollar on their book sold in stores. Meaning, corporate gets a huge chunk of the money from a writer's idea and intellectual property. While I would love a book deal one day I currently wake up early in the morning—even on days I don't feel like going out in the streets—and sell my books. What I do requires discipline and focus. Appreciate, don't hate. I am my own boss, the CEO of my company and no one can fire my Black/African behind either!!! I work for me and I earn for me! I heard a sista the other day tell a young brotha selling his music CD that she has 4 kids to take care of and couldn't support him...**AS SHE LEFT OUT OF A GAMEWORKS STORE!!! NOW SHE DIDN'T TELL GAMEWORKS SHE COULDN'T PATRON THEM BECAUSE SHE HAD 4 KIDS! WE NEED TO PATRON EACH OTHER! JEWS PATRON EACH OTHER, ASIANS PATRON EACH OTHER. SO WHY IN THE WORLD CAN'T BLACK FOLKS REALIZE THAT WE NEED TO PATRON EACH OTHER?**

5. **WE MUST STOP FEEDING OURSELVES AND OUR CHILDREN JUNK FOOD!!!** Pop, chips, candy...none of it is good for you in the long run. Start cooking at home, making salads a part of the meal plan, drink water, make your own juice **(CUT OUT THE KOOL AID)** and eat healthier; if you don't eat healthier, one day when you are older and your health has failed, the doctor will restrict what you can eat anyway and put you on a ton of medicines that will have more bad side-effects than helpful effects...or you might die! I know too many of us on dialysis right now! Drink water. Alkaline is excellent for the body and it taste spectacular. Cut out the pop and koolaid! Like one conscious sista said, what is kool aid anyway? A bunch of chemicals! When you see how third world countries struggle just to find clean water it makes you wonder why us Black Folk don't appreciate what we have in our own faucets.

6. **WE MUST STOP SPENDING ALL OUR MONEY ON WEED, THE CLUB, LIQUOR AND CLOTHES (AND IF YOU'RE A FELLA, ADD HOES TO THE LIST!!!)** It is bull. We as Black

folks spend so much we could probably crash the economy if we stopped spending for three days!!! The club ain't paying your bills! The liquor ads and companies don't even know your first name. Ed Hardy and Deron and Baby Phat and Dickie and the latest pair of Jordan's don't care about you; you are just dollar signs to designer brand companies!!! Sistas laugh at me when I say no matter how much money I make, I will continue to shop for deals. But a lot of them are on Section 8 and rocking expensive clothing. I'd rather have a house and wear less expensive clothing than rent and "be sugar sharp," as the old folks say, and be broke! There's nothing wrong with looking good but it's all about priorities and Black Folk, many times our priorities are all out of whack!

7. **WE NEED TO STOP TALKING ABOUT "MY BABY MAMA" "MY WIFEY" AND THE LIKE. GET MARRIED!!! HAVING A TON OF KIDS AND NOT BEING MARRIED IS NOT CUTE!** We don't have the Black family any longer. No family=No Community. Men need women and women need men and children need both parents.

8. **STOP TALKING ABOUT "I'M SAVED" WHEN YOU HAVE BEEN IN AND OUT OF JAIL AND STILL SELL DOPE...IN YOUR OWN COMMUNITY AND ROB YOUR OWN NEIGHBORS!!!**

9. **WE MUST LEARN HOW TO READ, WATCH BBC NEWS AND LISTEN TO NATIONAL PUBLIC RADIO FROM TIME TO TIME!!! STAY ABREAST OF WHAT IS HAPPENING AROUND YOU!**

10. **WE NEED TO READ UP ON EGYPTIAN HISTORY AND TRUE AFRICAN HISTORY!!!** Some of the bibles going around are not the real bible. The research to prove it is out there. What we as the Black American population have been reading is what has been given to us by White slave masters. Why do we trust anything given to us by those who enslaved us? That is a question I have always wanted to know regarding Black people... Sidenote: I heard on the news that the Catholic church is currently trying to take out the passage that states that Jesus had wooly hair. Think about that...what makes you think they haven't been changing the bible all along. Reading

the bible is good but one must make sure they are not reading one that has been altered.

11. **WE MUST STOP THINKING THE PREACHER IS THE ONLY SOURCE OF WISDOM!!!** Spiritual guidance can be a great thing but sometimes the preacher is swindling the church, crooked within his own personal life or informally biblically educated. We must stop putting all our trust into one man or woman. There should never be a time when one feels that they cannot question something a preacher has said. Yet, within the Black community we oftentimes give preachers superhuman status and allow them to lead us astray at times! Not everything said by a preacher is correct. Do your own research! In Nigeria preachers are telling their congregation members that their children are witches and need exorcisms. These Nigerians are believing these preachers and giving them all their money to perform exorcisms on their children. It has now gotten to the point where children have been disowned by their families, communities and churches and have been killed or tortured by family

members who believe their children are witches! Also, there have been numerous cases wherein Catholic priest have molested African boys and when the African boys tell their parents, their parents have pleaded with their children to deal with the sexual abuse since the priest are revered as men of God and because the priests have promised the parents their sons will go to school to further their education. Don't think it's only happening to Africans. The same issue is occurring right now in every hood in America when it comes to giving some of these preachers unduly power and say-so within our lives. A good example is this: When Hurricane Katrina occurred, many preachers told me personally that I should not worry about "those people because they have history deeply stemmed in VooDoo." These are Black preachers. They said God let that happen to them because they were evil. Something is wrong when people do not have empathy for other human beings who are suffering. Already the government turned their backs on Hurricane Katrina victims, how can we as Blacks afford to do the same to our own? Then I heard another preacher on television say the same thing—

that *those people*, the Hurricane Katrina victims, were believers of evil and false religions. Well, I personally think it is *evil* for Black preachers to say such nonsense! When does a Black person's life count? And if a Black life doesn't count to another Black man who is supposed to be of God, what is the world coming to? How does this link to preachers sometimes misleading people? Well, I have heard many a Black person, the educated included, lament the same sentiments: that the Hurricane Katrina people only got what they had coming to them for not being believers! These Negroes were apathetic to their own Black brothas and sistas because of what their preachers had taught them. Not all the Hurrican Katrina victims were unbelievers. Whenever we can take a blanket statement such as that of the aforementioned preachers and become unsympathetic to the individuals involved, that is scary. It is thinking like this that can cause people to commit terrible atrocities. When will we ever learn to use our brain and think? That's what I want to know!!! Those preachers had no business saying that mess but their followers should have been able to use their brains and realize that it was mean and not of God to say Katrina victims deserved what happened to them. (Also, look at that Eddie Long situation—I'm just sayin'!).

12. **WE MUST STOP SAYING THERE'S NOTHING ANYBODY CAN DO TO CHANGE OUR COMMUNITY!!!** We all can help halt the problems within the Black Community. With this attitude, we are not taking accountability for our own actions. Mexicans took one day and did not go to work to show America how much we need them. Well, SINCE WE AS BLACK FOLKS IN AMERICA SPEND MONEY LIKE IT'S GOING OUT OF STYLE, WE HAVE THE POWER TO GAIN POWER IN AMERICA--IF ONLY WE WOULD WORK TOGETHER! IF NONE OF US SPENT ANY MONEY WITH ANYONE NON BLACK/AFRICAN FOR TWO DAYS AND DID NOT GO TO WORK, THE US ECONOMY WOULD PROBABLY CRASH AND COLLASPE!!! THEY (CORPORATE) DEPEND UPON THE BLACK DOLLAR!!! WHY DO YOU THINK NASCAR IS STARTING TO FOCUS ON ADVERTISING TO BET AND WITHIN THE BLACK MARKET??? BECAUSE THEY REALIZED HOW MUCH MONEY THEY COULD MAKE OFF

BLACK PEOPLE, THAT'S WHY!!!!

13. **BLACK WOMEN STOP BEING SO MEAN TO OTHER BLACK WOMEN!!!** Older and younger Black women can be so rude, mean and spiteful to one another. And furthermore, stop stealing each others men as well! Brothas aren't as disrespectful towards each other the way sistas are to each other at times.

14. **WE MUST STOP CALLING OUR CHILDREN BAD!!!** No other race that I know of call their own offspring bad as much as Black folks. What you say is what you get. And you are cursing your kids when you say such things. And STOP CURSING OUT YOUR KIDS!!! IT IS JUST WRONG!!!!

15. **YOUNG GIRLS....STOP SELLING YOUR BODIES DIRT CHEAP!!!! IF YOU WANT TO BE A WHORE, GO TO PLAYBOY OR THE BUNNY RANCH AND GET THE PROPER PAY.** I, for one, am tired of seeing young girls out talking about how a guy paid them $30 or $250 for sex when I am out selling my books. Let's do better than that. Your body is sacred. You can hold another human

being in your body. That is a blessing. Treat your body as a prize and a blessing.

16. **WE NEED TO STOP SMOKING WEED ALL DAY!!!** Grow up. Read. Start a business. Get a visa and a passport and travel internationally. There are plenty of other ways to pass time and enjoy life. Smoke if you want (I personally like wine, that is my vice) but there should never be a time when wine or weed or anything is more important than learning and earning something!!! Work, go make your money. Don't sit around the house all day smoking weed.

17. **WE HAVE TO STOP LISTENING TO BS RAPPERS THAT TELL US IT'S COOL TO BE STUPID!!!** Gucci Mane is not stupid but in one song he says his mother wanted him to be a lawyer but he'd *rather sell them bricks*. Gucci Mane ain't selling nary one brick! He is too busy cavorting with White chicks at industry parties and in the studio making the next song for Negroes to blast that nuisance all over the hood. (Me personally? I looove "4 in tha Morning" with him and Trey Songz BUT! I am not listening

to all that mess all the time and I am not trying to live my life like a Gucci Mane song. A lot of these kids out here listen to this mess then try to live it out. Then we wanna go around crying about how bad the kids are these days. Part of the problem is the music and bad parenting!)

18. **STOP WRITING/READING ONLY HOOD BOOKS!!!** We see enough ghetto mess in the streets. Start reading history books, books about culture and science fiction and political reads. Then maybe we can evolve as a people... The more I think about it, we need to do more than just read a variety of books. We need to listen to wider genres of music. I'm talking about old school jazz like Thelonious Monk and Charlie Parker and world music. We need to take a break from all the rap and overtly sexual R & B ballads and listen to some classical music from time to time. Go to an orchestra house. We need to step our feet out of our hoods and see other things. Broaden our horizons...

19. **STOP GOING TO JAIL!!!! I'M SERIOUS!!! I'M TIRED OF MEETING 23 YEAR OLD BROTHAS WHO HAVE ALREADY BEEN IN JAIL FOR 30**

DAYS OR MORE. It's not cute. It's tragic actually. But WE, BLACK FOLKS, ARE THE MOST RELIGIOUS AND CHRISTIAN BUNCH...YET WE ARE SOME OF THE MOST REPRESENTED IN THE UNITED STATES JAILS AND STUCK IN POVERTY. Start having families and community and businesses!!!! Because what we are doing right now is not working!!! (Spirituality is important—very important—but a lot of times the political endeavors are involved in the churches. Many seeking to enter office give speeches at churches in order to garner votes. And in the beginning, the KKK backed Christian churches and did not even want Blacks to be members of Christian churches). I meet so many Black people that tell me they don't want to be Afrocentric. Unless some major changes are made within our community, within our mentality and unless we start owning thriving businesses, we lose. I don't believe God wants the Black race to continue to be on the losing end. Sometimes I think we as Black Folks use religion as an excuse to not do anything about our current conditions--as an excuse to be lazy. We need to do what it takes to change this state of Black emergency!

20. **BLACK WOMEN!!!! STOP THINKING YOUR SONS ARE TOO GOOD FOR EVERY GIRL THAT CROSSES THEIR PATH! AND STOP BABYING YOUR SONS!!! LET THEM BECOME MEN!** Some of y'all treat your sons better than your boyfriends and husbands!!! A young man is supposed to leave father and mother and cleave to his wife, not stay up under his mother's breasts for the rest of his life. Let your sons grow up and move on and be men.

21. **LEARN THE NEW LAWS THAT THEY ARE PASSING!!!** And not just that, fight, protest against laws that take away our rights!!!

22. **WE MUST STOP SAYING SLAVERY IS OVER SO WE DON'T WANT TO DISCUSS IT WITH OUR CHILDREN!!!** Many Jewish kids 5 years and older knows something about their history and Hitler. But us Blacks, we say slavery is over and do not want to discuss it with our children. We are doing ourselves a great disservice. You have to know who you are and where you came from in order to know where you are going. I keep stressing

this point for a reason: Why do you think the Jews are as far as they are? They own things, have money, are well connected...**AND THEY NEVER LET ANYONE FORGET WHAT WAS DONE TO THEM!!!** How quickly us forgiving Negroes are...much to our demise. The affects of slavery are prevalent today...yet we don't want to talk about it...(shame, shame, shame on us Negroes/African Americans/Blacks!) and on our dollar bills, the founding father's, who were just as terrible as Hitler, the founding fathers are on all of our dollar bills. The one on the twenty-dollar bill, Andrew Jackson, okayed the slaying of over 800 Native Americans and was a part of our ancestral enslavement. I read that after they, the colonists, killed the Native Americans, they cut off the Native American's noses for their kill count. Jews would not allow Hitler to be on their currency... Just a thought.

23. **WE MUST START GIVING BETTER CUSTOMER SERVICE!** Whether you own your own business or work for someone else, do better on the customer service end. I patroned a sista's healthfood store

the other day and her service was terrible. Her prices were ridiculous, service was slow and she had the nerve to be snotty. But then I found another Black owned health food store and their service was phenomenal. When service is bad, find another Black owned business to work with, don't just say Black service is terrible and patron everyone but us. Yet and still, there is no excuse for us Blacks in business to give terrible service.

24. **WE MUST STOP PATRONING PLACES THAT COOK SOUL FOOD BUT ARE NOT OWNED BY US!!!** These places are popping up all over the place, non Black owned soul food joints. I used to love South Side Soul Food in Chicago and Harold's Chicken until I realized that these places are selling my culture's food and even though they have some of us in there cooking, we don't own the place! **Why on earth would we allow anyone to come into our hood, open up a place of business that cooks our own food, have us cook it while they make all the money off the business!** You don't see us cooking Greek food and owning the restaurant! You don't see Blacks owning

Italian restaurants and you will never see one of us own an Italian restaurant while the Italians do all the cooking! If one of us did have the nerve to open up an Arabic or Italian or Greek restaurant you'd be darn sure they would never work for us and cook their own food while we made all the money! And they'd never patron the restaurants either! Yet I see tons of brothas and sistas going in and out of Nu Wave Chicken and Fish in Detroit on 8 mile. I want to picket that place so bad. But none of that is necessary. If Black Folks said, "NO, YOU CANNOT COME INTO MY COMMUNITY AND SELL MY FOOD TO ME AND HAVE ME WORK UNDER YOU!" they wouldn't do it to us! This is strictly our own fault.

25. **SISTAS, DON'T JUDGE A BROTHA BY HOW HE DRESSES OR HIS CAR, JUDGE HIM BY HIS HEART AND HIS ACTIONS!** I know some thirty-something sistas talking about they won't talk to a guy wearing South Pole or that they can't stand a man that dresses like yada, yada, ya. Never do they say, I won't date a man who hits me or I will only date a spiritual man who has his head together and has goals and is family

oriented. I would like to hear more sistas talk about finding men who will be awesome husbands rather than what color eyes a man has or what kind of shoes he sports or what kind of car he drives! Not that a man shouldn't have his stuff together—he should. But his personality and spirituality and heart should matter just as much so.

26. **ON KWAME—AND YOU KNOW I HAD TO GO THERE!!!** Never have I heard so many Black Folks call the radio stations and go off on one man. All these listeners were going on and on about how they hated Kwame and what he did to his city and how he ought to pay the city! It wasn't enough that the media publicly lynched bruh, naw. We had to turn around and help sock it to ole boy, too. Question: how come none of us sistas and brothas called in to the radio and complained about what Bush was doing under his regime?!!! While we were busy bitching about that brotha Kwame, they were passing all kind of laws right under our noses. But none of us have called in on the radio all day and griped about any of that Tea Party mess either. So why the

heck did we do that to Kwame! Once again, Blacks slamming another Black! I can't respect us for that. If you can complain on Kwame, then open your mouth up and complain on all these other government officials who are taking your rights away and forcing you into neo-slavery. When the higher ups take away your rights, you are their slave. ...How quick a Black is to cut one of his own!

27. **...AND ABOUT THEM LACEFONT WIGS!!!** They don't look right! The fake hairline looks like that of a plastic barbie doll. And they will eventually mess up your hairline; so basically right now they are selling you something to cover up your own hair that will in a few years tear up your hairline and make you need some sort of Alopecia hair treatment. If you don't believe you are beautiful sistas, there are many beautiful Black women who are not afraid of their own hair—and look darn good wearing what is naturally theirs! Back in the days before slavery, Africans were proud of their hair and they wore styles that let you know which tribe they belonged to. Upon their arrival to America, slave masters and the

colonists shaved all their hair off which left them embarrassed. This embarrassment is something most of us have never overcome. I used to wear weaves too. I wanted locks years ago but did not do it until 2007. A few years ago I had sistalocks and could not believe how many brothas and other races of people were digging it. I don't know if the sistas have been too brainwashed to believe their own beauty or what, but we need a **Beauty Revolution**. And I'm going to do my best—my very best to start one. I'm telling young Black kids they are beautiful everyday; I'm telling grannies with fros they look good; I'm telling brothas with locks that those locks are banging. Somebody's got to do it!

28. **Complain In Classy Fashion!** When you get bad service, don't start acting all ghetto and curse out the employee with everyone watching (and have onlookers thinking, *this is how ignorant Negroes act*). Rather, play the game the way they play it and efficiently: contact corporate and complain in a calm manner. Get the employees name who caused the problem and report it to the company manager and the corporation.

I wrote this because I love Black Folks, but many of us are really becoming ridiculous and embarrassing. The way some of us act we might as well be in 1710 because we are diving backwards. We need to take the necessary steps to create positive change within the Black race! ...Don't shoot the messenger!

Important things to check out:

Zeitgeistmovie.com (watch the movie)
Infowars.com
Professor Griff (formally of Public Enemy) Youtube Illumanati Take Over of Hip Hop
Read the book Sacred Woman by Queen Afua
Read the Michigan Citizen Newspaper
Learn more about Marcus Garvey
Watch Kwame Ture videos on Youtube
Take African Studies, Sociology and Urban Studies courses at a University to better understand yourself, your community and world
Read The Miseducation of the Negro by Carter G. Woodson
Watch the Malcolm X biopic
Watch the Josephine Baker biopic (notice how the NAACP did not help her when Baker was accused of being a communist)
Tupac (Killuminati on Youtube)
Read Langston Hughes Simple Story Collections
Read The Norton Anthology of African American Literature
Read The True Power of Water by Masaru Emoto
Read That Hair Thing by Dr. JoAnne Cornwell

What Black Women Need To Know!!!

...Having a healthy, fulfilling love relationship takes dedication and work no matter who you are but with 70% of Black women being single in 2010 and 42% of Black women remaining unmarried, it is time for some of us sista girls to make some changes...

Scenario I

I was at a gas station a couple of months ago. I saw this real pretty darkskinned chick at a gas station. There was this darkskinned brotha who pulled his car behind the gas pump she was parked at. He told her she was fine and tried to holla at her. She just kept ignoring him and acting like he was invisible. Then, he got a little more brave and pulled his car closer to her. At this point ole girl straight up cursed the mess out of dude. It was embarrassing. All the other dudes at the gas station watched on. A few smirked. I myself was embarrassed for ole boy. And I had to shake my head at the chick for behaving like that.

A few years from now, after a consecutive run of bad relationships, this same chick is gonna be going around telling everybody, "Black men ain't no good." Or that "Black men don't like Black women." Or, she'll be the same bitch complaining every time she sees a Black man with a non-Black chick. All she had to do was tell dude thank you but that she was unavailable. All that cursing a brotha out was so unnecessary and out of pocket.

Now on the other end, some brothas do pull some crazy shit on women and I will get into that in a minute. But not all brothas are bad. What it is is that a lot of us Black women are sleeping on the good ones or not picking up on the signs when a brotha is bad for us.

Scenario 2

I was having a conversation with this one cute darkskinned buddy of mine. We got on the subjects of relationships—which, you know are my thang—lol. Well, she was saying she was ready to dump her current boyfriend. So I asked her why. She said he was too controlling and a big baby; he didn't want her going clubbing as much as she did, he didn't like her girlfriends, he was a homebody and that he was ready to get married but she wasn't sure whether or not she wanted to get married. Now girl, is hitting on forty, has kids and has never been married and says she has been both father and mother to her kids. Question: why are you still not ready to get married at almost forty and so in love with the club? Next question: why would you want to dump your man because he does not like your friends? Final question: how can you be both father and mother to your kids unless you created them by your self, with no invitro or anything?

This whole situation is ridiculous and I have not been able to get her to look at the whole picture. The guy is a nice dude and faithful to her and loves her enough to marry her. A lot of dudes don't even want to get married. So why doesn't she treasure the fact that he loves her enough to want her as his wife? And a man that's a homebody? Oh, that should never be an issue. At least he's not hanging in the streets and at least he is home. And as far as him not liking her friends? None of her friends would dump their men if one of their men didn't like her!

Then you have that new movie Nsecure. Oh, what bull! I didn't even go see that shit. The previews were enough to me. From what I saw on the preview all it was was a bunch of Black women with supposedly controlling Black men... And then you have the one Black woman asking the other Black woman why she is staying with her man when he is so insecure.

First of all, when you are in a relationship you do have to answer to the other person—having to answer to your spouse does not make him or her insecure. Secondly, all this being independent shit is not what's up. Did you know the Rockefellers started Women's Lib to tax the other sex and get the women out of the house so that they could brainwash children at an even earlier age (preschool)? It was not to ensure equal rights for women. It was all about money and the elite controlling the masses. All these bullshit ass songs about a woman being independent and not needing a man—have you noticed they target that shit to urban radio? You don't hear all that on more mainstream stations. Then Nicki Minaj was on The Wendy Williams Show and said, when Wendy asked her if there was a love in her life, that her only love is named Benjamin Franklin. I have no problem with Nicki Minaj and realize she is being controlled and actually, she does have a boyfriend. But why do the Black female celebs always have to say they are single and focused on their career? Wendy was co-signing that shit and said that a young woman in her twenties should only be concerned with making her money. That is incorrect. Yes, young ladies should focus on attaining an education or owning their own business or having a career but love does not have to be thrown out of the window for career's sake. Just look at the country singers and whatnot. They get married at an early age and, whether they get divorced later on down the road or not, you don't hear the media pushing them to only focus on their money.

There is an attack on the Black family. If we have family, then we have a community and we grow stronger. Don't be fooled by the current status quo of all this “be an independent Black woman” jazz. I am a feminist—well, better yet, a neo-feminist and what that means is that I am a proud woman/queen. I do need my king. We work together. We build together egalitarian style. Sometimes I have to concede to his wishes when he is right, sometimes he has to listen to me when I am right. I take care of the in house stuff i'm good at. I can cook and clean but at the end of the day, he has no problem cooking either or massaging my feet. All this not needing no man is not correct. And you can nurture your household and still have a career. I do it all the time. Shit, Wendy Williams is doing it and works with her husband as well—he was her manager!

Here are a few helpful hinters. In conjunction, please read my novel ***Even If You Don't...*** and also pick up ***Vert Means More Than Green: Very Explicit Real Talk*** wherein there is excellent, detailed relationship advice.

1. **Keep a clean house—all these young girls living in squalor is not what's up, straight up! You have got to clean your house!**

2. **Learn how to cook healthy meals for your family and man.** Learn how to cook. I don't care what they say, real men like women that can cook! If you don't know how, that's okay. Get your grandmother or someone you know who knows how to cook to teach you ten classic meals.

3. **Take some classes in subjects that interest you at a community college.** Community colleges are affordable and the knowledge can help you evolve as a woman. Stagnation is not a fulfilling lifestyle.

4. **Stop aborting your kids.** Don't have sex with someone you don't want to have a kid with. This is your child, your seed. All these abortion clinic commercials aka planned parenthood are just ways to decrease the Black race. Do you know a lot of rich Caucasian elite actually specifically donate money that allow Blacks to attain birth control and abortions at low cost? They do it for a reason: **THEY DON'T WANT YOU TO CONTINUE YOUR BLOODLINE!** And all that birth control is not good for your body. Depo is blowing the sistas up something awful. And not having a period for months is

not natural. Don't mess with Mother Nature's natural flow.

5. **Practice being sweet to your man.** Give him compliments when he does something nice. Tell him how much you love him. If you don't, someone else will.

6. **Quit putting your mama and your homegirls in your relationship!** Either they don't have a man or they will give you advice they themselves would never follow. Only listen to them if they themselves are in good relationships and are not hating on yours and if the advice is reasonable and the advisor is candid about their own relationship mistakes.

7. **If a guy is not a drug dealer or a baller or paid out of his mind, so what!** Many times these type are dogs anyway. Go for a dude who is motivated, working on his goals, trying to get a house (or already has one), wants to be married, spiritually in tuned with your spiritual beliefs and kind to you.

8. **Just because a guy is ugly does not mean he is going to treat you well.** Actually a

whole lot of nice looking brothas don't even think they are good looking and act kinder and nicer towards women than the ugly dudes act towards women. Choose a man you are attracted to. Part II will go more in depth on this topic.

9. **Learn how to garden.** They are starting to get rid of seeds. All these genetically modified foods—like seedless grapes and seedless watermelons. That is not how nature intended it. In a minute you won't even be able to grow real food when they stop selling the actually seeded fruits and vegetables. I personally do not know how to garden but this is one of my own goals.

10. **Love yourself.** Don't be worried about what another chick has and don't be the one always gossiping about everybody else. Work on you. Love you and the rest will follow.

11. **Love yourself enough to walk away from a man who is not good for you.**

12. **Set standards for yourself.** Don't have a man just for the sake of having a

man.

13. **Don't date a man who is under your league.** It doesn't work. He will start dogging you out and try to give you low self-esteem to make himself feel as though he has brought you down to his level.

14. **If a man does not inspire you to better yourself and make you a better person, leave him alone.** It doesn't matter how fine he is or how much he money he makes, leave him alone if you do not feel better within the **relationship.**

15. **Ask your man what he wants from you and be willing to sit down and listen and take his wishes to heart.** If he can't stand you clubbing three times a week, stop. A lot of times women cannot handle the truth about themselves. Then they want to go around saying they were the perfect one in the relationship and that their ex was the problem. That is not always the case. A lot of women fuck up their relationships. Unfortunately, I know I've messed up in a good relationship before.

16. **Have a give and take relationship.**

Don't have your hand out, always looking for a man to give you money and to pay your bills. Find out what you are good at doing and figure out a way to earn income with it. But don't you be that one paying the tab day one on the first date or paying the tab all the time, either!

17. **Set goals and aspirations for yourself.** Don't just sit around the crib on Aid and welfare and section 8 and shop and wait for a prince on a horse to snatch you up and save you E-40 style. A real man is going to detest that shit. And the ones that like these type of women, pick fine, model types to cash out for a few months before they move to the next one. Replaceable is the key word here. The only other way this works out is you get a dude who cons you into thinking he is going to save you only to realize a few months later that he is using you for a place to stay and looking to you to pay the bills via your government assistance while he sits on the couch all day, smokes weed and watches ESPN.

18. **Don't curse your man out in public.** If you have a problem with something he says or

does in public, tell him in private. Let him be a man and allow him his dignity.

19. **Let go of pettiness and let the attitude go.** Some Black women are always frowning and complaining about something. Let it go. Do things that make you happy. No one wants to be around a woman who is constantly unhappy and difficult to please. Be peaceful, don't always start arguments. At the same time, you are not a doormat to be walked all over either. You don't have to put up with riduculousness! But all that arguing and yelling mess is old and will not make for a healthy and loving relationship.

20. **Be quiet sometimes.** Give his ears a break. I am a talker but I have learned to be quiet and listen to my man at times.

21. **Don't think because you can fuck or give good head that that is all that's required to maintain a good relationship with your dude.** Sex is important and it will do you a world of good to be good in bed. But: men can find plenty of other good pussys and some of them will no doubt be better than yours! You can learn how to be better

sexually and even have a man whipped but if you don't know how to be a good woman outside the bedroom, you are not going to be able to "keep" your man. I hate the phrase "keeping a man." What you have to do is maintain a healthy relationship. You can keep a dog or goldfish. Men you don't keep. You work with your man.

22. **Being pretty is not going to make your man stay with you either. You have to have something going for yourself.** There will always be another pretty woman. And pretty with a stank attitude will get you nowhere.

23. **Don't hit a man.** Women think they can hit a dude but that he should not hit them back. Now, back in the day? I did fight a dude but he hit me first...So...Long story... And I have never had to fight with another dude since.

24. **Watch your mouth.** Watch what you say to your man. They have feelings and get hurt by things women say also. Recently I said something straight up out of pocket to my dude and I said it more than once so I'm

working on making it up to him. It's better to not say the BS in the first place but should you find yourself saying some terrible mess to your man, apologize and treat him special and get him to forgive you. Us women can say some f-ed up things too; it's not just men that can use words as weapons.

25. **No matter what people say about you as a Black woman, no matter how the media tries to portray us, know that you are an awesome woman.** Hold your own esteem high.

26. **Always trust your initial gut feeling on a person.** If you do not like someone, do not talk to him, do not take gifts from the person, do not take money from him and do not go anywhere with him, do not even hang out with the person out of sympathy or for friendship.

27. **Many times men become angry with a woman if they have liked her for years and she has not reciprocated their feelings.** If a guy has been obsessed with you for years yet you never really liked him,

don't one day decide to date him. They may turn violent if you do finally decide to date or they may secretly resent you and that leaves a lot of room for foul play!

28. **Never allow anyone you have just met or someone who is mad at you to bring you a drink or food.** Let the food come from the waitress at a restaurant and watch the bartender pour the drink. **DO NOT ACCEPT PACKAGED FOOD WITH THE SEAL BROKEN FROM SOMEONE YOU HAVE JUST BEGAN DATING!!!**

29. **If you think you have been the victim of a date rape drug, tell someone and go to the nearest hospital immediately. One of the drugs, GHB leaves the system after 72 hours.** Ketamine leaves the system after only 12 hours. These drugs can be easy to attain. **DO NOT LEAVE YOUR FOOD OR DRINKS AND RETURN TO THEM. TAKE YOUR DRINKS TO THE RESTROOM WITH YOU AT CLUBS AND DO NOT LEAVE YOUR FOOD UNATTENDED—EVEN AT A RESTAURANT WHEN OUT ON A DATE—DON'T EVEN GO TO THE RESTROOM AFTER YOUR DINNER HAS BEEN SERVED WHEN**

OUT ON A DATE!

30. **Just because you have known someone for years does not mean they will not slip a date rape drug on you.**

31. **Listen to what a person says when initially dating or getting to know him or her.** If they have never had a serious relationship, are unduly angry at the opposite sex, exhibit strange or anti-social behaviors, if you find they are constantly deceitful and constantly lying or never want to meet your friends and family, LEAVE THEM ALONE!!!

32. **Never go out of town with someone you have just met or just began dating.**

33. **Never go out of town with someone who is angry with you!**

34. **Pay attention to a person who jokes about date rape drugging people or goes into detail about how to make such drugs at home.**

35. **NEVER, NO NEVER DRINK PREMADE DRINKS AT PARTIES OR CLUBS. NEVER DRINK**

DRINKS PREMADE AND LEFT OUT IN PUBLIC UNATTENDED OR ATTENDED (whether or not you know the attendant), PUNCH BOWLS ETC.

For Our Brothas!!!

...In America 72% of Black babies are born to unwed, Black mothers. Many of our young Black men are headed to prison or the city morgue when they should be in college. But in 1980, before crack was introduced to urban America, more Black men where in college than in jail. I wrote this article to try to probe into the problems that lead our brothas astray and to give simple yet viable solutions to the current problems Black men face today.

In the media and on the streets brothas get it hard. Not as hard as Black women but you all do get the short end of the sterotyping stick in many instances. Still, everybody wants the Black man. You are respected in sports and in whatever field you decide to soar in, be it entertainment or on the streets. But there are some things you all need to do/work on in order to have better functioning lives and to help promote a better community within Black America.

1. **Brothas need to read.** I am so tired of brothas telling me they don't read. There is so much hidden knowledge in books. Pick up nonfiction books, autobiographies, newspapers like Native Sun or Michigan Chronicle and read!

2. **Spend time quality with your kids.** Yes, child support is terrible these days the way they take funds out of brothas checks when the child's mother is on the system and that is unfair because the child barely gets any of the money after the state gets their cut. Going to jail for nonpayment of child support is also not a good thing. But none of that is your kid's fault. Spend time with

your child no matter how trifling his or her mother is. Remember, you laid down with that woman and created that baby.

3. **Wear a condom.** Especially if you want to avoid #2. Sometimes y'all be stuffing y'all privates into anything raw and that's just nasty.

4. **Drive without the liquor in a plastic cup.** I don't get that plastic cup thing. Seems like you'd come out better putting your liquor in an unsuspecting McDonald's beverage cup instead of those tell-tell plastic cups from the liquor store. Regardless, it's not a good idea to drink while driving anyway. You can seriously hurt someone or yourself and if that isn't enough encouragement to stop, think about the problems you'll have if pulled over with liquor in your lap.

5. **Selling drugs is so 1980's.** Find another means of earning a living. This is why so many of our brothas are in jail instead of in college. You'd come out better working at Whitecastle's instead of being a cheap corner crack seller. And your life would be less endangered.

6. **Get your license issues straightened out.** There are way too many brothas out here with suspended licenses.

7. **When you find a woman you can trust who is good to you, keep her and don't cheat on her**. What goes around comes around. You can be a player all you want but one day when you get old, you're going to need someone around to take care of you. If you mistreat the good one, you're going to suffer. It doesn't take five or six women to make you happy. Find the woman who is everything you want and need and treat her right. Men who are married live longer than those who don't marry. It's a proven statistic.

8. **Don't listen to everything your mother tells you in regards to women.** Follow you're own gut instinct on the woman of your choice. I don't have any kids yet so I hope I don't do this: many mothers don't want their sons to be with any woman who will be a permanent fixture in their son's lives. I think subconsciously they fear their son won't be there as much for them. Or

that they will somehow become number 2 in their son's lives. But honestly, the bible says you are supposed to leave father and mother and cleave to your wife, not your mama. It's good to love your mother. I'm close to my mother. But your wife should never have to play second fiddle to your mother. That's not the way it's supposed to work after you turn 18. I have even heard mothers tell their sons to date numerous women instead of sticking with one woman and remaining faithful. As long as you are with other women instead of one, you aren't in a serious commitment. Unfortunately, a lot of women treat their sons like their husbands. And it's a two-fold thing because many times your mother has control over you (the kind of control she can't have over her husband) and at the same time your mother will feel as though she has companionship with you. I see this so much it's crazy. Women who can't let their sons go and grow on their own. It's not good. It's actually a handicap because the mama's are not allowing their sons to have a functioning relationship with a woman, which is how God created it. I know so many women who can't stand their daughter-in-laws and it's a shame because back in the day, they probably had the same problem with their own mother-in-law's. It's a vicious cycle that needs to be stopped. I hope I don't do that to my sons.

9. **Don't try to find a chick you can move in with and take advantage of.** Get yourself together. Get your own place and car. Work on your own career. Part of this problem is being spoiled too much by a mother who treats you more like her husband than her son. Then you go looking for a woman to take care of you like your mama did when in actuality, you are supposed to take care of your woman financially and work together with your woman regarding finances. You are not supposed to live off a woman without bringing anything to the table.

10. **Don't fall for that Miss Indepence mess!** You need a woman you can work with who is more than willing to work alongside you. People need each other. Men need women and women need men!

11. **Put a little romance into your lady's**

life. Don't stop with the romance after you feel like you've got her; don't get too comfortable. Give her a card just because. Bring her flowers when she isn't expect it.

12. **Learn how to communicate with your woman.**

13. **Learn how to sweet talk to your woman.**

14. **Before you do something, think of how you would feel if your woman did it to you and think of how you would feel if the shoe was on the other foot.**

15. **Listen to your woman when she gives you good advice.** Don't always look at it as nagging or your wife/woman trying to mother you!

16. **Don't chose a woman based on her butt circumference.** Look for a good woman who will be loyal to you. Looks are important but if this is all you look for you'll be in child support court telling the judge what a rat your babys mom is. Just because

she has a juicy ass does not mean she will make a good mother or wife.

17. **Go to college.** Unless you are in sports, business, real estate or entertainment, there's no reason you should not be educating yourself. Low paying jobs when you actually could be doing something better with you life is not what's up!

18. **Travel.** Get out of the hood and experience life. Some people in Detroit have never even been to Canada. Now that's a shame! Traveling will help expose you to the world. There's nothing worse than being limited mentally. Get a passport and check out places that interest you. There is way more to the world than your hood.

19. **Watch your drink when you're out.** I have heard too many cases of people being slipped something while out with so-called friends. One lady told me her nephew was slipped horse tranquilizer and that he has never been the same after that situation. That is one of the most horrible things I have heard. First of all, where would

someone get horse tranquilizer? Secondly, *why* would someone do that? So be careful when you're out and drinking.

20. **Don't look for the common route when choosing a career.** It seems like everyone is into real estate these days or selling bootleg cd's or trying to rap (which is okay if you're good at it). But why not try something different? If you have a hobby that is something you enjoy, why not try to do something career-wise with it. If you like fixing things up around the house, why not start a handy-man company? If you are creative, and like using your hands, why not go to school for sculpting. If you're into wearing T-shirts why not start a novelty T-shirt company? There are other things you can get into other than the typical, run of the mill popular trend that every other brotha in the hood is already doing. Lately every dude in the hood is on the same hustle. Step outside the box.

21. **Stop being a gossip!** Society tries to act as if it is just women who gossip and start mess but being out selling books in the streets I hear so many men tell all their

business and their wives' business on their cell phones or to other dudes out on the street. Stop telling personal business when you are out and about.

22. **Stop the senseless killing!** Nowadays it seems brothas don't fight anymore—they just pull out guns. And guns equal death. Stop trying to prove how hard you are with a gun—especially when being hard can get you killed. Or in jail.

23. **Have a strong sense of self-esteem.** Lots of brothas have low self-esteem. No matter who you are, remember: someone loves you. You are loved.

I love my brothas. You all are sexy, spiritual, wonderful and the very essence of Blackness. I hope this article gives you helpful hinters that will make your life a bit easier.

Please Check Out Our Other Books

Even If You Don't…

Everything In Style Should Not Be Worn

Just Talking To You: My Journal & Other Outrageous Things

Vert Means More Than Green: Very Explicit Real Talk

Kamikaze of Songs

Like Garden Eyes Coming Soon!

mianneAbooks.com
Flippynerds.com
LightsOnFoundation.org

Email Any Comments Regarding This Book To:
mianne@mianneAbooks.com

www.ingramcontent.com/pod-product-compliance
Ingram Content Group UK Ltd.
Pitfield, Milton Keynes, MK11 3LW, UK
UKHW040013200726
13854UKWH00001B/179